Original title:
Branches of Solitude

Copyright © 2025 Creative Arts Management OÜ
All rights reserved.

Author: Matthew Whitaker
ISBN HARDBACK: 978-1-80581-736-9
ISBN PAPERBACK: 978-1-80581-263-0
ISBN EBOOK: 978-1-80581-736-9

Conversations with the Hidden Foliage

In the shade of leafy chats,
Squirrels giggle, hide their snacks.
A raccoon with a hat so grand,
Debates with trees on soft earth's stand.

Whispers float where shadows tease,
With every rustle brought on breeze.
A wise old owl chimed in the fun,
'Things are brighter when the day is done.'

Forgotten Trails in the Quiet Woods

Lost paths where the mossy stones,
Snicker softly, greet the bones.
A hedgehog on a lonely quest,
Claims he's the woods' very best.

Vines that tickle passing toes,
Clowns of nature with funny bows.
Each twist and turn, a laugh that peels,
As laughter echoes 'round the wheels.'

Secrets Weaved in Natural Silence

Mice in whispers plot a scheme,
To steal the pie from dreams' sweet cream.
The trees roll eyes like seasoned stars,
While crickets drum on rusty jars.

Bubbles burst from the brook's delight,
Fish joke about their flashy plight.
In silence, secrets full of cheer,
Tickle the leaves till the night is near.

A Solitary Dance of Shadows

On the stage where shadows play,
A lonely dancer sways in gray.
He trips on sticks and claps so loud,
Until the fireflies form a crowd.

Each twirl's a giggle, each step's a jest,
As shadows partner with the best.
An audience of critters cheers,
For the one who dances with no fears.

A Retreat Into a Thousand Leaves

In a grove of laughter, trees tickle the sky,
Squirrels in bow ties, they prance and they fly.
Leafy whispers gossip, oh what a scene,
Nutty debates held in leafy cuisine.

The branches are dancers, waving so free,
While the shadows take selfies, oh look at me!
Sunbeams are jesters, playing wild tricks,
Nature's own comedy, with all of her quirks.

The Chime of Distant Wrens

Wrens in the distance, they chirp out a tune,
Singing 'bout food like it's their big boon.
Fluttering about with a flair so divine,
Caught in their gossip, I sip my red wine.

A pop and a flutter, a flip and a twirl,
These feathery drama kings make my heart whirl.
Chimes of their chatter roll soft through the air,
I can't help but chuckle; it's quite a rare affair.

The Lure of an Empty Clearing

An empty clearing calls, a dance floor for ants,
Where daisies wear hats and the sunshine does prance.
Invisible parties where shadows delight,
And frogs croak like jazz bands under the night.

The grass squeaks with laughter, the blue sky takes bets,
On who will fall first in hilarious sets.
Nature's own stage where the world seems so light,
Who needs a punter when the bugs take flight?

Caught Between Silence and Shadow

Caught in the hush where the whispers collide,
The pines start a giggle; oh what do they hide?
Bats dabble in mischief, there's laughter in flight,
As crickets tell jokes deep into the night.

Echoes of chuckles bounce off every tree,
While owls squint their eyes to see what they see.
It's a riot of stillness, a delightful scare,
In realms of the quiet, humor's everywhere.

Reflections in a Starlit Lament

In the mirror of night, stars do shiver,
The moon's a giggler, a celestial river.
Here I dance with shadows, silly and bright,
Who knew solitude could sparkle with light?

Whispers of laughter escape from the trees,
As if they share jokes with the lightest of breeze.
I chuckle at crickets who croon with delight,
While the owl rolls his eyes at my clumsy flight.

When Shadows Grow Long

The sun takes a bow, oh what a long day,
My shadow elongates, it's starting to sway.
'Don't trip over me!' I shout with a grin,
As it trips over rocks, oh where have you been?

When dusk drops her curtain, I dance like a fool,
With shadows as partners, we break all the rules.
We twirl and we spin, till the stars come to play,
And my shadow insists on leading the way.

The Last Leaf of Autumn's Wane

A leaf clings on tight, but not for long,
It flutters and giggles, hears its own song.
Falling in slow-mo, a comedic scene,
While squirrels watch on, their faces turn green.

"Oh give it a rest!" the last leaf did shout,
"I'll twirl to the ground, I'll laugh, that's my route!"
With a flip and a flop, down it goes with a cheer,
The squirrels just roll over, "We knew it, oh dear!"

Hushed Conversations with the Moon

At midnight I chat with the moon by my side,
"Are there cheese-filled craters?" I teasingly bide.
It just winks back, with a chuckle so bright,
"Only if you bring crackers to share for the bite."

The stars snicker softly, eavesdropping near,
While the clouds play hide and seek, giggling in cheer.
"Oh moon, let's discuss all the dreams that we've spun,
And how sporadic my hair looks on the run!"

Silence Cradled in Nature's Lap

In the woods where whispers play,
The trees giggle in a breezy ballet.
Squirrels steal acorns, their stealthy creed,
While mushrooms might ponder, will they succeed?

A brook chuckles softly, it skips with glee,
As frogs croak praises to the buzzing bee.
Leaves toss their heads, a joyful spree,
In nature's own chorus, everyone's free!

Rooted in Stillness

The old oak stands still, a wise old chap,
While ants host meetings, all under his cap.
A turtle ambles, slow as a rhyme,
And birds hold gossip, all in good time.

Grasshoppers leap with a comedic flair,
As daisies blush bright, unaware of the stare.
Nature's ball, where awkward's a trait,
Is a riot where silence plays 'wait and mate'!

Contemplation by Candlelight in the Glen

By candle glow, the fireflies wink,
As shadows prance, while crickets think.
Mossy cushions form a comfy seat,
Where squirrels juggle acorns, a comical feat!

The breeze tells tales of a lucky snail,
As candles melt slowly, an enchanting trail.
In the glen's embrace, humor's discreet,
Each flicker of light adds to nature's beat!

The Solitary Journey of a Wandering Leaf

A leaf floats down on a breeze so grand,
Dancing through air, a whimsical band.
It twirls past branches with playful grace,
And lands on a toad, who looks out of place!

The leaf chuckles soft while resting awhile,
As critters join in for a nature's style.
With laughter and joy, they spin and weave,
In this merry tale of a wandering leaf!

Shadows Danced on Corkscrew Trails

On trails where shadows play,
The squirrels dance, go their way.
They spin and twirl in a jig,
Competing with a fat, round pig.

The trees lean close, all in cheer,
Whispering secrets for us to hear.
A raucous laugh from a bright green frog,
Who thinks he's the king of the log.

A rabbit hops with a silly grin,
Waving at the sun and the wind that spins.
It's a comedy of nature's delight,
Where each creature vies for the spotlight.

Did you see that clumsy bear?
He tripped on his toes without a care.
Yet laughter echoes through the grove,
In this wacky, woodsy world we rove.

The Velvet Silence of Nature's Heart

In the hush where critters play,
Silence wraps the world today.
But wait! A chipmunk's cheeky shout,
Breaks the peace, there's no doubt.

Crickets serenade the trees,
Each note tangled in a breeze.
A porcupine spins disco dreams,
In the quiet, nothing's what it seems.

The deer prance in with poise and grace,
While a wise old owl smiles from his place.
He chuckles softly, with knowing eye,
As the stars wink at the night sky.

The velvet night breeds mischief too,
When raccoons plot their little coup.
In whispers bold, the night they'll steal,
Making moonlight their grand meal.

Cradle of the Wistful Whisper

Beneath the rustling leaves so bright,
A tiny mouse has taken flight.
He dreams of cheese, in a daze,
While ants march by in funny ways.

The wind tells tales of distant lands,
While butterflies dance with dainty hands.
A gopher laughs in his little den,
Planning a party—come, bring a friend!

The brook giggles as it flows,
Filled with tales and tiny woes.
"Why so glum?" asks a dragonfly,
"Stick with me, you'll learn to fly!"

Oh, the whispers wrap around us tight,
In cozy nooks, everything feels right.
Under each leaf and open sky,
Nature laughs, how can you deny?

Living in the Threnody of Trees

Underneath the leafy fray,
The trees hum tunes in a quirky way.
A parrot croons a silly song,
While the woodpecker taps along.

"Life's a jest!" crows one tall pine,
"Come share in my humorous shrine!"
A lizard winks, his colors bright,
As he basked in the morning light.

Even the shadows laugh and tease,
With every breeze, they stir with ease.
A raccoon with a mask so sly,
Throws shadows at a passing fly.

So here we dance through sunlight's beams,
Amid the thrumming of giggling dreams.
In the whimsical grove we live, you see,
It's all in fun, just you and me.

The Isolation of Misty Mornings

In the fog, I lost my way,
A squirrel stole my breakfast tray.
Caught in mist, I took a pause,
And wondered if my cat had paws.

The coffee cup, it sat, untouched,
While raindrops danced and lightly clutched.
I chuckled at my morning fate,
As shadows played with my breakfast plate.

The world seemed blurred, a silly sight,
I tried to wave, but lost my light.
A bird flew by, it gave a wink,
I laughed so hard, I spilled my drink.

Yet in this haze, I found my cheer,
A dance of joy, or maybe fear.
For solitude's a playful jest,
In morning mist, I felt so blessed.

Unseen Footsteps on Lonely Trails

On paths where no one dares to stroll,
I heard a giggle and lost control.
Who's this ghost that walks with me?
A figment of my wild esprit?

The leaves they rustle, a laughter echoes,
I think I see my own two shadows.
They prance about, chase after ducks,
In solitude, I'll take my luck.

A tree leaned in, it shared a joke,
With every twist, new laughs bespoke.
I paused to listen, grinned with glee,
Nature's comedy, who needs TV?

Through lonely trails, I trip and hop,
With unseen friends, I never stop.
In solitude's grip, a dance I find,
The joy in silence, delightfully kind.

Twilight Beneath A Weeping Elm

At dusk, beneath a droopy tree,
I whispered secrets to a flea.
It hopped around, a tiny muse,
In twilight light, we sang the blues.

The branches swayed like silly hats,
I watched a squirrel, meditating on mats.
"Is that your best?" I shouted loud,
It twitched its tail, quite proud, then bowed.

The stars blinked down, they rolled their eyes,
As shadows waltzed beneath the skies.
I chuckled while the wind took flight,
Oh, sweet solitude, you feel so right!

But in this glow, I felt a jig,
The elm just laughed, and I danced big.
In quiet times, the humor grows,
With every breeze, the laughter flows.

The Quietude of Echoing Silence

Silence sang a silly song,
With echoes where I thought I'd belong.
A whisper teased me, "Take a seat!"
I laughed at how my thoughts compete.

In quietude, the air was thick,
I wrote a note and gave it a flick.
A paper plane flew past my head,
I wondered where the pigeons fled.

As time went by, oh what a prank,
The stillness roared, a hidden flank.
The quietude, it tickled my mind,
In solitude's space, such fun I find!

So here I sit, with giggles near,
In echoing silence, I shed no tear.
For when alone, I find my muse,
In laughter's glow, I'll never lose.

Waiting for Dawn Amidst Twilight

The clock ticks slower than a turtle,
I sip my tea, it's becoming a hurdle.
The walls start to lean, my chair loses fight,
I smile at shadows pretending they bite.

The moon's got jokes as it hangs in the sky,
Whispering secrets with a wink of an eye.
Dawn takes its time, as if making a plan,
While I ponder if I'm still a real man.

The Solitary Song of the Whip-poor-will

Oh whip-poor-will, your tune's kind of odd,
A mix of a croak and a very sad plod.
You sing to the stars while I just tap dance,
In hopes that one day, I'll find my romance.

I chuckle at branches that scratch at my hair,
They swish with the wind, looking quite debonair.
Yet here I stand, all alone in the wood,
Singing to critters, oh, if only they would!

An Ode to Untrodden Paths

A path yet untraveled, a fork in the way,
I trip on my thoughts, but hey, who can sway?
Each step feels like dance, but my feet only stumble,
Finding new ways that make my mind tumble.

The bushes all giggle when I lose my grace,
They nudge one another, it's quite the fine space.
I wave at the trees, do they wave back to me?
Or is it just my wild imagination, you see?

Memories Amongst the Silent Thorns

Amidst all the thorns, sweet thoughts start to poke,
I laugh at the prickers, they tease like a joke.
With memories mixed like a soup in a pot,
Some tasty, some bitter, I forget them a lot.

But oh, what a feast of the laughter we'd share,
When the prickle-filled moments turn light as the air.
So here's to the thorns, that prickle and scratch,
They guard all the smiles, and they all have a match!

Solitude Among the Arbor

In a park where shadows play,
I chat with squirrels every day.
They nod in solemn agreement,
While I spill my deepest lament.

A leaf dropped down, it made a sound,
I laughed, it seemed so profound.
My jokes fall flat on ears of bark,
Yet trees stay laughing in the dark.

The wind whispers secrets of glee,
But only the bench talks back to me.
I crack wise with the rustling grass,
While daisies snicker as they pass.

So here I sit, with oddball friends,
Our chats and chuckles never end.
In this woodsy jest, I find delight,
Who knew solitude could be so bright?

The Stillness Between the Leaves

There's a gap where giggles creep,
A stillness where the shy ones leap.
I joke with crickets in the night,
They chirp back, it's quite a sight.

The leaves are eavesdropping all day,
On my banter and what I say.
A branch sways, as if to tease,
I bow to them with utmost ease.

The silent air, a comical friend,
Hangs around, it won't offend.
I share my puns with the moon's soft glow,
And laugh when the stars blink back in a row.

In this stillness, humor blooms,
With nature filling up the rooms.
Who knew the silence would bring such fun,
With jokes that rival the morning sun!

Paths Worn by Silent Footfalls

These trails are trodden by feet unknown,
Each step a whisper, a funny tone.
I make small talk with the wandering ants,
While leaves giggle in their leafy pants.

The rocks are grumpy and odd, you see,
They grumble back at my banter with glee.
I tease the path for being so slow,
While flowers smirk, they always know.

Among these ways where quiet is keen,
I wear my chuckles like a sparkling sheen.
I wave at the bushes, they nod with mirth,
Together we jest, for what it's worth.

So I walk on, a lone funny guy,
With paths that chuckle as I pass by.
In silence, I dance, and the world can't see,
How laughter sprouts from my solitude spree!

In the Embrace of Twilight Trees

As dusk unfolds in hues of gold,
I meet the trees, both strange and bold.
They whisper stories in playful tones,
Of fairy romances and dancing cones.

The twilight wraps me in gentle grins,
While shadows stretch, and laughter spins.
I share my punchlines with the breeze,
And the branches roar back, "More, please!"

Each rustle between the branches' sway,
Is a sign that humor's here to stay.
I bow to the trunks, they applaud my flair,
As fireflies flicker like stars in the air.

Amidst this twilight, bright and free,
I've found a home in hilarity.
So here I linger, where giggles please,
In the embrace of this forest of trees.

Unspoken Stories of the Forest

In the woods where secrets creep,
Squirrels gossip, but can't keep.
Acorns laugh at the rusty old tree,
While a shy twig hums silently.

The mushrooms dance with polka dots,
Giggling softly in their tiny spots.
A deer tells tales to a sleepy log,
While frogs croon under the morning fog.

Leaves chuckle as the wind sings,
Dancing lightly, casting rings.
Foxes wink, thinking they're sly,
In their world, the trees are the sky.

Beneath a canopy of chuckles bold,
Lies a realm of laughter untold.
Nature whispers with a careful grin,
A riddle wrapped in a leafy skin.

The Lonesome Song of Pine

A pine tree croons its solo tune,
Under the watch of a lazy moon.
Its needles sway, a creative twist,
In the forest, it feels quite missed.

The squirrels tap dance in delight,
While the branches request a hug, tight.
'Why so lonely?' asks a cheeky crow,
With a wink that's meant just to show.

Pinecones sigh at the silly scene,
Elkhorn shadows plotting in green.
The breeze interrupts with a playful shout,
'You're a star in this woody bout!'

So the lonesome pine continues to sing,
Embracing oddness, the joy it brings.
In its solitude, a party's begun,
Each whisper of wind is a laugh, a pun.

Hollow Echoes of Forgotten Roots

In the earth where laughter hid,
Roots stretch wide, but they are bid.
A turnip claims it has the best tales,
While beetles boast of epic gales.

Rabbits gossip, perched on a stump,
Telling tales that make others jump.
Old roots hum a nostalgic beat,
While toadstools wiggle, a spree of sweet.

The echoes dance in the soil's embrace,
Tickling memories in a secret place.
A worm twirls, it has no shame,
Digging deep for a funny name.

So let's dig down for chuckles piled,
In the depths of dirt, innocence wild.
With humor hiding in every little twist,
The forest's laughter can't be missed.

Beneath the Weight of Silent Boughs

Underneath the leafy dome,
Critters gather, far from home.
A raccoon flips through a magazine,
While shadows dance, all serene.

The branches stretch with so much care,
Holding secrets, whispers in the air.
A chatty squirrel bets on the breeze,
While lizards lounge on mossy trees.

Woodpeckers drum a lively beat,
Tickling branches, oh so sweet.
A frog does yoga on a stone,
In a quiet world, yet never alone.

Beneath weighty limbs, laughter swells,
Each shrub a sage with stories to tell.
Nature's humor wraps all around,
In this quirky home, wonder is found.

Garden of Hollow Echoes

In a garden where whispers roam,
The flowers giggle, no one's home.
Bees dance solo, no buzz about,
While shadows chat, then twist and pout.

A rake leans back, taking a nap,
While weeds just plot their grand escape.
The sun winks down, what a sight!
Who knew solitude could be so bright?

A gopher's joke, a turtle's snore,
Each critter laughing at the door.
Pigeons strut with their heads held high,
In this empty space, oh my, oh my!

So if you hear a chuckle near,
It's just the plants sharing their cheer.
In this garden, where all are free,
Laughter blooms as a sight to see.

The Specter of an Unseen Companion

A ghostly friend, with sneakers on,
Paces beside me from dusk till dawn.
He cracks jokes in the chilly breeze,
And trips on shadows like it's a tease.

We share snacks, though he's quite a tease,
He vanishes when I wish for peas.
Haunting my heart with a playful grin,
His presence is felt, though he won't win.

In moments quiet, he makes me laugh,
Turning my sadness into a gaffe.
An unseen buddy, ever so sly,
Throwing popcorn at the passing sky.

Though he's a wisp, he's never bland,
In whispers, he sprinkles joy like sand.
So here's to the friend who's a bit out of sight,
In our world of giggles, we both delight!

Faces of Solitude in Autumn's Light

In autumn's glow, leaves wear grins,
Whirling around in a dance of spins.
Squirrels chuckle, hiding their loot,
While pumpkins bounce, all cute and astute.

The trees play tricks with their leafy caps,
Trying to lure in unsuspecting chaps.
But here in silence, smiles arise,
With every rustle, we share sly eyes.

Nuts tell tales; acorns drop by,
Each glance feels like a comedic high.
A crow crackles, a far-off joke,
As sunlight beams, the laughter awoke.

So stroll through this land of quiet cheer,
Where solitude sings, yet all draw near.
In leaves that tumble, in breezes that sway,
The faces of joy won't fade away.

Where Time Meets the Tattered Shadow

Time tickles softly, wearing a hat,
It plays peek-a-boo with a friendly cat.
Shadows stretch, then prance away,
While clocks giggle, oh what a play!

Tattered whispers loop like a rhyme,
Tracing old stories, defying time.
A worn-out chair whispers back,
With memories held in every crack.

The sun snores softly, dreaming bright,
As shadows chuckle in fading light.
A dance of silence splits the seams,
In this space, where laughter gleams.

So pause for a moment, drink it in,
Where time meets mirth, and joys begin.
A tattered shadow, a giggle's embrace,
In solitude's realm, we find our place.

Stories Carved by Time's Hand

In the garden that's overgrown,
Squirrels debate in a tone,
About who has style, who has flair,
While robins judge from their chair.

Old benches groan with each tale,
As the ants dance, they prevail,
Chasing crumbs under the sun,
Life's a game that's meant for fun.

A clock ticks slowly in the shade,
While sleepy cats plot their trade,
Napping through hours lost, confused,
In dreams, they solely get amused.

Every leaf whispers a jest,
Nature's humor, the very best,
Laughter lingers in the air,
Silly moments, a joyful flare.

Unraveled Threads of Evening's Calm

Under a sky made of seams,
Fireflies weave in and out of dreams,
Chasing shadows, a jig of light,
While frogs croak jokes under the night.

The moon winks at the stars' delight,
As owls hoot in comic sight,
One says, "Who?" – and starts a trend,
Enjoying the buzz that won't quite end.

Crickets strum a funny tune,
Tickling fancies 'neath the moon,
While grasshoppers boast of their grace,
In this concert, there's always space.

Evening sighs with a gentle tease,
As breezes flit through rustling leaves,
In this laughter, we find our balm,
Unspooled moments in evening's calm.

The Endless Night's Gentle Caress

In velvet shadows, the mischief brews,
Cats in capes play superhero blues,
While weary stars spill sleepy wine,
A twinkle here, a sparkle fine.

Sidewalks glow with stories vast,
As whispers of secrets from ages past,
Night's a cradle, rocking with glee,
Comfort found where no one can see.

A moth flirts with the porch light's dance,
While crickets clutch their sole chance,
To serenade all the lazy pups,
Who dream of chasing their big, silly ups.

In this world, all worries fade,
As shadows shift in the masquerade,
A laugh escapes from the gentle press,
Of night's embrace, the sweetest mess.

Paths Where No One Treads

In the woods where the oddballs roam,
Trees hug the wayward, far from home,
A squirrel pastes on a triumphant grin,
As raccoons plan a cheeky din.

Mushrooms gossip about the rain,
While frogs sip tea, a curious gain,
Whispers of paths beyond the seen,
In this corner, all things glean.

Caterpillars parade with flair,
A fashion show in the open air,
Bugs critique the latest place,
"Who wore it best?" becomes the chase.

While owls share puns, soft and sublime,
In these realms, all flow like rhyme,
A dance of quirks in solitude's light,
Paths untraveled, a comedic sight.

Traces of Solitary Winds

In a park where the lone balloons float,
A squirrel debates, should he wear a coat?
Trees gossip softly with a rustling sound,
While my lost thoughts play hide-and-seek around.

An ant holds a meeting with three tiny friends,
Over crumbs of a sandwich, their laughter transcends.
A gust whispers secrets, tickling my cheek,
I chuckle at nature, so coy and so bleak.

A breeze steals my sandwich, it swirls and it twirls,
While I chase my own thoughts, around like girls.
The shadows grow longer, the sun starts to yawn,
It's just another amusingly lonely dawn.

I tie myself up in a twisty old vine,
As laughter erupts from a stuttering pine.
With every odd giggle, I find what I've sought,
A comedic connection in solitude's plot.

A Dance of Dried Petals

Beneath my feet, a parade with no rhyme,
Dried petals wave back, a fluttering mime.
They dance in the breeze, oh, what a sight!
As I step lightly, it feels so polite.

A ladybug winks, giving me cues,
To join in the fun, to laugh and to lose.
Together we twirl in a chuckle-filled spin,
In a ballet of blunders, no way to win.

Drifting along in this silly charade,
I trip over roots that the trees have portrayed.
Yet giggles erupt from my heart's silly throne,
In this land of the lonely, I'm never alone.

So twirl on, dear petals, in your comical campaign,
For each rustling whisper echoes joy through the pain.
And as laughter cascades from the old wooden bench,
I remember that solitude can be quite a wrench!

Solace Amongst Forgotten Woods

In woods where the sun forgot how to play,
A butterfly murmurs, 'Is it night or day?'
Trees stretch their arms, but none seem to care,
While shadows do jiggles, unaware of the air.

I stumble upon mushrooms, wearing funny hats,
They gather in circles, those whimsical brats.
A rabbit with glasses, reading a map,
Lost in the chapters of his afternoon nap.

The whispering leaves have their own little jokes,
As I laugh with the owls, those soft-spoken folks.
With every odd rustle, a riddle they weave,
In the woods of the lonely, there's much to believe.

So I'll toast with the toads and recount all my dreams,
Underneath the moon's grin and the day's silly beams.
In forgotten places where solitude weaves,
I find laughter's comfort, and joy never leaves.

Navigating the Thicket of the Soul

In the thicket of thoughts where the wild things bloom,
I fumble and tumble like a peacock in gloom.
Twigs tickle my ankles, a mischievous test,
Who knew reflections could be such a jest?

A spider weaves wonders while cracking a grin,
Though I'm stuck in the branches, feeling chagrined.
The thorns make a jest of my peculiar dance,
As I trip through the brambles in a ludicrous prance.

Frogs croak encouragement from their comfy spots,
Dozens of snickers from all strange little dots.
With a chuckle and giggle, I swing through the mess,
Finding laughs in the chaos, I settle for less.

In this deep tangled forest of whimsical grace,
I've learned that solitude's not a dark, dreary place.
With laughter embracing me, I carry my role,
Navigating the thicket, I'm whole in my soul.

Waiting by the Distant Stream

A rubber duck floats by, quite a sight,
It quacks at the fish in a swimmy plight.
I wave to a frog, it just croaks in reply,
It's a chatty affair, but where is that pie?

Clouds overhead look like marshmallow fluff,
The breeze whispers jokes, but they're never enough.
I toss in a pebble, it makes quite the splash,
And all the fish giggle—what a silly bash!

Sitting here waiting, my snack's gone astray,
A squirrel scampers past, doing acrobat play.
I thought I was patient, serene as a dream,
But time ticks by slowly by the distant stream.

So here I will stay, with my dodgy old shoe,
A muse for a poem that's funny yet true.
I'll laugh with the ripples, and sip from my flask,
Waiting here endlessly, is that too much to ask?

The Melancholy of Fallen Petals

Petals drift down, dressed in pink and white,
They gossip about bees, what a silly sight.
A voice in the breeze says, 'Do you see that tone?'
'The rose thinks she's fancy, but she's all on her own.'

A snail slides by, thinking he's quite the chap,
He carries his house, but takes a quick nap.
The daisies debate, who's prettier, and how,
While the leaves just roll their eyes—oh, the drama now!

Yet in this small garden of laughs and sighs,
It's hard not to chuckle at the butterfly lies.
With each fragile flutter, they claim they can dance,
But trip on their wings—it's like a bad romance.

So here's to the petals, both bright and forlorn,
In laughter's sweet cycle, no need to be worn.
For in each toss of color that flutters and sways,
Lies a joy that's contagious, cheering up gloomy days!

Fragments of a Wandering Soul

I wandered the woods with a map made of cheese,
The squirrels all laughed, as they blew on the breeze.
I followed a trail of giggling leaves,
But got lost in a maze of old honeycombs' thieves.

The sun was a beacon, but also a clown,
Winking at shadows that danced up and down.
A ghost made of giggles popped out from a tree,
It said, 'Hey, you lost it? Just follow me, free!'

Through thickets of laughter and nibbles of bread,
I stumbled on mushrooms with hats on their head.
'This way is a route where the lost always roam,
But I'd rather find pizza, and just go back home!'

Though fragments I gather from paths that I rave,
Each twist brings a chuckle, and oh, how I crave!
This wandering spirit with a whimsical mind,
Finds joy in the journey and all that I find.

Hidden Music in Quiet Places

Under the old stairs, I hear a faint tune,
It's a ruckus of whispers from dust bunnies' swoon.
They dance to a melody, soft yet absurd,
While the carpet complains, 'Have you heard what I've heard?'

A teapot is boiling, but curiously sings,
It hums of adventures and whimsical flings.
In shadows, the spoons perform tap-dancing feats,
While the coffee cups clack in the old kitchen beats.

Behind every door, there's a joke to be found,
Like socks having parties, all mismatched and crowned.
The fridge hums a ditty, off-key and unsure,
As the leftovers giggle, 'We can't take much more!'

In quiet places, the music won't cease,
Each creak and each clatter brings laughter—no peace.
So let's join the chorus, and dance with delight,
For life is a tune that sparkles so bright!

In the Heart of Still Woods

In the woods I sit and stare,
A squirrel's dance, a comical fair.
He chases shadows, slips on dew,
Mistaking dreams for nuts, it's true.

A rabbit hops, a real charmer,
His ears flapping like a drama.
I can't help chuckling at their glee,
Nature's circus, just for me.

The trees gossip with the breeze,
Whispering secrets, if you please.
A bird sings out a silly tune,
Even the fungi seem to swoon.

I toast to laughs in nature's den,
A comedy show with furry men.
So here I'll stay, no need to fret,
In the woods, I'm the best audience yet.

Solitary Reflections on Nature's Canvas

A canvas stretched, oh what a sight,
The clouds are paint, the sun's the light.
I try to sketch with nature's brush,
A masterpiece but makes me blush.

The fish in the pond make quite a fuss,
Splashing about, they ride the bus.
While frogs croak tunes of a random jam,
Nature's band plays—thank you, ma'am!

A butterfly flutters, strutting its stuff,
Confidently prancing, oh so puffed.
I giggle as it lands on my nose,
A ticklish feeling, who would've known?

In solitude, I find the fun,
Where nature's jesters play and run.
Each leaf a laugh, each stone a grin,
A silly world where joy begins.

The Cry of a Distant Nightingale

A nightingale sings from afar,
But the sound's more of a rusty car.
Its tune, it seems, got stuck in bad,
Yet still it chirps, and I can't be mad.

Meanwhile, a hawk does a high dive,
Chasing its lunch like it's alive.
The rabbit, quick, does a dance of woe,
While I laugh so hard, my sides nearly blow.

A critter pops out from a shrub, quite bold,
Thinking it's hidden, but it's looking old.
With a wiggle and jiggle, such a grand show,
Even the stars start to sparkle below.

Nature's a stage with whimsy galore,
With actors and actresses, who could ask for more?
I sit and chuckle, cup of tea in hand,
Absorbing the humor as laughter unplanned.

The Sigh of Swaying Branches

Branches sway with a lazy grin,
The trees gossip, "Where have you been?"
A breezy day with a gentle tease,
Rustling whispers among the leaves.

Woodpeckers tap a rhythmic beat,
While ants march by on tiny feet.
I join their parade with a goofy sway,
A woodland dance in a clumsy display.

The shadows stretch and play hide-and-seek,
As sunlight tickles the ground, so meek.
I trip over roots, a laugh I can't fight,
Nature's own slapstick afternoon delight.

So here I am, in my funny plight,
Amidst the woods, filled with pure delight.
The branches sigh, sharing their cheer,
In this silly silence, I'm happy here.

The Emptiness of Unwritten Tomes

In my mind, a library sits,
With dust on all the empty bits.
The pages shout, yet none can see,
Oh, what a thrilling mystery!

I sent a letter to my brain,
But it returned with 'Not again!'
The stories that I thought were great,
Are lost to time and endless fate.

A hero fights, but what a joke,
His sword's a spatula, just smoke!
In lands where minds refuse to roam,
I write alone, in my new home.

The tales I weave are all for laughs,
Like wobbly legs on wooden giraffes.
So join me here in this delight,
Where unwritten tales take flight at night.

Secrets Held by Distant Echoes

Whispers travel, light as air,
Through valleys deep, without a care.
They bounce around in playful jest,
While I just sit, a secret guest.

The echoes giggle, tap my shoulder,
Telling tales of skies grown colder.
A cat in boots leads on the chase,
While I'm just lost, with no good grace.

They speak of dreams that went awry,
Of spaceships made of pumpkin pie.
But who would dare to take a peek
At laughter hidden in the bleak?

So listen close, and share the fun,
With echoes dancing in the sun.
The secrets murmured, soft and clear,
Are giggles shared, and joy sincere.

The Forgotten Bloom of Winter's Chill

In frosty fields, the flowers sigh,
A tulip wearing a winter tie.
They laugh at snowflakes as they fall,
'Is this a dance? Come one, come all!'

With frozen roots, they joke and jest,
'We bloom when winter's at its best!'
The sun forgets to shine its light,
Yet blooms dispute the chill of night.

A cabbage turned into a queen,
With icy jewels that gleam and sheen.
While carrots wear their frosty hats,
And sing along with winter's chats.

So raise a glass to blooms in snow,
Who frolic where the cold winds blow.
For even in the coldest strife,
There's laughter found in winter's life.

Rustling Leaves of Nearing Dusk

Leaves rustle softly, what a sight,
Like giggles shared at dusk's twilight.
They gossip low, beneath the skies,
While crickets sport their evening ties.

The breeze joins in, a playful friend,
Tickling trees around the bend.
With every crackle, every sway,
It whispers secrets of the day.

A squirrel jumps, with acorn plans,
While shadows stretch and make new fans.
They cheer him on, a lively crowd,
As he declares he's brave and proud.

So dance with leaves, and sing out loud,
For twilight brings a playful shroud.
Amidst the rustles, secrets soar,
And laughter lingers evermore.

Solitary Pathways Unveiling

In a forest where nobody dares,
The squirrel debates how much it shares.
A leaf sneezed, a twig mocked the breeze,
And shadows chuckle, doing as they please.

Alone in the woods, a raccoon slips,
Dreaming of honey and marshmallow dips.
The trees gossip, with roots intertwined,
While the mushrooms giggle, oh so unrefined.

The path twists, a route all askew,
A lost shoe is laughing, what's next to ensue?
An owl perched, wearing spectacles tight,
Says, "I feel lonesome – is that a delight?"

Yet the thorns wink, in glee, they embrace,
For solitude's party has plenty of space.
So dance, little critters, in glee and in jest,
For alone can sometimes mean simply the best.

Echoes from the Hollowed Tree

A hollow tree giggles, oh what a sound,
Echoes of laughter bounce all around.
Inside it resides a very shy gnome,
Who swears he won't trade his roots for a dome.

The woodpecker's knocking, a beat that's absurd,
While the squirrel narrates, it's quite the weird word.
A twig stands up, shouting, "Look at me!"
Yet nobody's there – just a bumblebee.

The raccoons gather for a long discussion,
About which snack creates the finest hush-tion.
The owl critiques while sipping his tea,
As the frogs croak choruses, feeling carefree.

From within the walls, echoes arise,
Chortles of the unseen, much to their surprise.
In solitude's clutch, they find such delight,
Turns out being alone is just out of sight.

The Lonesome Bough's Song

Up high on a branch, a lonesome bird hums,
While ants plan a party, over a few crumbs.
The wind giggles past, asking questions galore,
"Why's everyone so quiet?" They're pondering lore.

A stumped old log starts moaning a tune,
Sharing its woes with the light of the moon.
A worm pops his head, says, "Why so glum?"
"I'm just feeling heavy, like a beat-up drum!"

The shadows hold secrets of jokes they won't share,
And critters concocting their own little fare.
A distant coyote howls in delight,
As the moon raises an eyebrow, laughing bright.

Yet solitude wraps them in a blanket of cheer,
Where awkward is normal, there's nothing to fear.
And the lonesome bough sings, not quite on key,
But it's funny to see all this glee set free.

Veils of Abandonment

Under leaves of despair, a snail takes a ride,
Wishing for friends, but keeping inside.
The shadows assemble, for a quirky soirée,
Where no one feels lonely, they giggle away.

A patch of lost daisies gathers some moss,
Debating on royalty, who's really the boss.
A butterfly flutters, with no one to boast,
So she whispers secrets through petals, the host.

In solitude's realm, a raccoon plays chess,
With a stick for a knight – it's quite a mess!
The cloud looks down, laughing soft in the blue,
At the splendid awkwardness, known by so few.

Yet in this bouquet of misfit retorts,
The joy of the hidden is as good as reports.
For the veils of abandonment, woven with cheer,
Celebrate the funny, year after year.

The Gentle Rustle of Isolation

In a room where dust bunnies roam,
The lonely socks find their home.
Crisp packets make crinkly sounds,
In silence, they spin tiny rounds.

A chair squeaks in a playful tone,
It wishes for friends, but stands alone.
The fridge hums a lullaby soft,
While the cat dreams of chasing a loft.

Worn-out books cover tales divine,
Of adventures far, but none do twine.
The clock ticks loud, as if to jest,
Mocking the stillness, it's quite the pest!

So here's to the whistle of quiet distress,
Where laughter blooms, albeit in jest.
Surrounded by echoes, I find delight,
In a cozy cocoon, just out of sight.

Yearning in the Shade of Oak

A squirrel dashes with grace unrefined,
Chasing acorns it hopes to find.
The oak tree chuckles, makes it a game,
'You'll be back here!' It shouts its name.

Beneath its branches, a picnic lies,
Where ants plot their sneaky surprise.
Napkins flutter, drinks spill with cheer,
Nature's slapstick, wait 'til you hear!

A breeze whispers secrets, crows caw reply,
"Why not take a nap? Just give it a try!"
But the ants have plans, a grand buffet,
Under the tree, they dance all day.

So here's to the oak, wild and bold,
In its shade, many tales are told.
Amid the antics, life's joys unfold,
In the dance between shade and stories retold.

The Quietude of Forgotten Pathways

Once ran a trail, bursting with cheer,
Now tangled in weeds, no visitors near.
Mismatched shoes stand still and forlorn,
Socks lost in nature, unclaimed, and worn.

A hedgehog snoozes, quite pleased with itself,
While mushrooms throw parties, no book on the shelf.
Whispers of gossip float through the air,
"Did you see the last hat?" "Oh, how it could wear!"

Old bikes rust gently, stories they tell,
Of kids racing home, with laughter that fell.
Now crickets chirp, enacting a show,
In this quietude, we all come to know.

A mystery lingers, where did they go?
A rendezvous waiting, beneath the bough.
Paths will be filled, just need time to heal,
Until then, we'll smile, oh what a wheel!

The Weight of an Empty Canopy

High above, the branches surely sway,
But below, I ponder and play.
A hammock swings, with not much to hold,
While solitude giggles, a secret untold.

The clouds drift by, like balloons in the sky,
They peek in my heart with a curious eye.
A squirrel takes flight, planted on air,
Chasing its dreams without a care.

Castles of leaves, where shadows do twirl,
Invite all the gnomes to give it a whirl.
Laughter erupts in the thicket's embrace,
As sunlight dances on each little face.

So here I lay, with nature in tow,
Beneath an empty canopy, spirits do glow.
With a wink from the leaves, I chuckle with ease,
In the weight of the moment, I find my peace.

Whispers in the Canopy

The squirrels are chatting up in the trees,
While I'm down here, begging for some breeze.
They gossip of nuts, and plan their next raid,
While I trip on roots in this leafy parade.

A bird just squawked, I think it was me,
Mimicking voices, with all of its glee.
I joined in the chorus, off-key and loud,
It flapped its wings, far away from the crowd.

The branches above are a real comedy,
With pigeons that strut like they own the marquee.
They wiggle and dance, not a care to be seen,
While I'm just a leaf, all alone in between.

If trees could chuckle, this grove would shake,
With laughter so hearty, it's hard to mistake.
But I sit below, as the sun starts to fade,
A joke in the making—yes, that's how it's made!

Echoes of a Silent Grove

In a quiet nook, where the shadows conspire,
The crickets are cracking some jokes by the fire.
They chirp about summers, the heat and the rain,
While I roll my eyes, finding humor in pain.

A frog croaks a laugh from his mud-spattered rock,
He's next up for stand-up, time to take stock.
With jokes about flies and a tale just for me,
I giggle so hard, I nearly can't see.

The owls hoot wise, or at least they pretend,
With wisdom like that, who needs a good friend?
But at least in this stillness, I've company here,
It's funny how solitude's broken by cheer.

Echoes of chuckles float up with the dusk,
This grove's not so bleak, just some laughter, no fuss.
As night wraps around, like a warm, fuzzy quilt,
In solitude's arms, a new giggle is built.

The Loneliness of Twisted Limbs

In a forest where odd shapes do sport,
Twisted limbs wave like they've lost some court.
It's a dance of the gnarled, a waltz gone awry,
I can't help but laugh as I ask, "Oh, why?"

A tree tries to stretch, but it's tangled in knots,
It whispers to bushes about human thoughts.
"Why stand so upright when you could just bend?
Life's like a rubber band—snapping from trend!"

The shadows laugh with me, as leaves start to sway,
Commiserating my oddness in a funny way.
With bark that's quite rough and limbs that won't yield,
These friends of my folly make loneliness healed.

So here in the grove, where the oddballs convene,
We're the misfits of nature, a peculiar scene.
Funny how twisted can bring you such glee,
When all of your friends are as twisted as me!

Shadows Beneath the Leafy Veil

Under the canopy, where the light feels shy,
Shadows gather round, and they chuckle nearby.
Somewhat like me, they're not one for show,
We joke about daylight but never let go.

The leaves whisper softly, "Is the grass really green?"
While shadows roll over, pretending to preen.
They share all their tales, draped in dim layers,
As I sip my tea, making inner debayers.

"Why do we linger in this sparsely lit glen?
To hide from the sun or to dodge all the men?"
A shadow remarked with a flick of its tail,
"Just pull up a seat. Bring your own leafy pail!"

So here we all sit, a shady brigade,
Embarking on laughter, our fears kept at bay.
In somber disguise, we find joy in the trail,
Under the cool laughter of shadows' own veil.

A Solitary Prayer Among Pines

Under the pines, I offer a plea,
To squirrels and birds, please hear my decree.
"Oh, fluffy-tailed friends, drop nuts at my feet,
Lest I starve here in silence, with nothing to eat!"

The pine cones fall, my wish they must heed,
Praying for puddings, and snacks I might need.
Yet the pines just chuckle, their needles they sway,
As I sit full of hope, not a treat on display.

So I shout to the shadows, with laughter and glee,
"Let's start a party! Just you wait and see!"
But the wind is the only one joining the fun,
Too shy to respond, still I dance just for one.

Amidst this green crowd, I've found my delight,
A solo soiree under silver moonlight.
With twigs for my guests, and leaves for my cheer,
I'll celebrate solitude, oh, what a weird year!

Solitary Raindrops on Dried Earth

A raindrop plops down, not a friend in sight,
It giggles and rolls, what a comical flight!
"Oh, why am I solo, on this cracked piece of clay?"
The ground cracks a smile, then dries up in dismay.

Another drop tumbles, joins in the dance,
"Let's splash around! Oh, what a strange chance!"
With puddles forming, the earth starts to hum,
But the sun sneezes loudly, saying, "Time to go, chum!"

The joy of a duet, now just a mere tease,
As I watch my lone raindrop float off in the breeze.
"Can't we stay longer? I've just learned to glide!"
But the earth has no answers, it's lonely inside.

Yet I find it amusing, this plucky little show,
Of drops in a race, with nowhere to go.
So I cheer from the sidelines, with all of my mirth,
For solitary rainfalls can brighten the earth!

The Stillness of Forgotten Days

In my dusty old chair, I sit and I sigh,
With memories swirling like clouds in the sky.
The echoes of laughter, they tickle my ear,
As I ponder the days that have drifted from here.

"Where did all the fun go?" I ask to the dust,
The cobwebs respond, with a quiet, soft gust.
Life's like an old cat, too lazy to roam,
Content with its nap on the couch of my home.

I dream of the ruckus, the chaos, the thrill,
But silence is golden, and gives me a chill.
The clock on the wall doesn't tick like it should,
Reminding me gently of times that felt good.

Yet in the stillness, a chuckle takes flight,
As I claim my throne, being king of the night.
For even in solitude, humor takes space,
In forgotten days, I've still found my grace!

Wisdom from the Swaying Fern

The fern sways and wiggles, so wise and so green,
As it whispers to me, in tones soft and keen.
"Why stress over branches when you've got your roots?"
It giggles at worries that cause folks to hoot!

"Life's just like rainbows, it bends and it bows,
So throw your dilemmas at squirrels with your woes!"
Its fronds start a dance, oh, what a sight to see,
And now I'm convinced, I should wiggle with glee.

The sunbeam dips low, whispers secrets untold,
As the fern shares its wisdom, it makes me feel bold.
"Get tangled in laughter! Just let the world spin,
For nothing's a struggle when you let joy come in!"

So I twirl with the ferns in sweet, playful sway,
Finding truth in their jiggle, brightening the day.
Amongst all the stillness, a chuckle takes flight,
Thanks to those wise fronds, I embrace the night!

Beyond the Tenderness of Echoes

In a world of quiet laughs,
Where giggles play hide and seek,
The echoes bounce off walls of moss,
Tickling the shadows and the meek.

Lone squirrels wear tiny hats,
Debating life over acorn snacks,
As they arm wrestle round the tree,
Counting wins on fuzzy backs.

Footsteps fall with gentle grace,
Slips and slides in lone embrace,
Trees chuckle with their knobbly barks,
Watching folks trip on unseen larks.

Clouds drift in whimsical minds,
Shuffling dreams with gentle winds,
In this echoing realm of cheer,
Solitude is a giggling deer.

Reflecting on the Whispering Void

In the abyss where echoes dwell,
Jokes reverberate—oh, what a spell!
Laughter whispers through the space,
Bouncing off the moon's cold face.

Crickets chirp in serious tones,
Discussing life with their little bones,
As owls roll their eyes from afar,
Saving punchlines for a shooting star.

Breezes carry tales untold,
A chicken crossed to find some gold,
Yet in the void, it tripped and fell,
Leaving giggles echoing in its shell.

So here we float on quiet streams,
Dancing lightly with our dreams,
The void knows laughter's perfect art,
A reminder we are never apart.

The Solitary Hourglass's Sands

Time trickles down with a sandy twist,
Each grain giggling as it's missed,
Turtles race past, out of breath,
Wondering who'll win their own death.

An hourglass sighs, tilted askew,
Musing how much can one snore do?
While shadows perform in the corner light,
Dancing with dust in a whimsical flight.

Watches tickle time with glee,
Cackling at clocks and their strict decree,
Sands tell stories—one grain at a time,
Who knew solitude could be so sublime?

Yet lonely sands seek a friend's embrace,
Teasing time to pick up the pace,
In this glass, giggles flow and blend,
Making solitude an unlikely friend.

Solitary Ambassadors of the Wild

The forest greets the solo critters,
Who send out invites to all the quitters,
An ant in a tux and a mouse in a tie,
Hold a council beneath the sky.

Dancing leaves have the silliest tales,
Of lonely whales and odd snails,
They giggle as they sway to the breeze,
During secret chats with the old trees.

A deer in glasses reads a book,
While shadows play the sneaky crook,
In solitude, they toast to the jest,
With wild rhythms putting them to the test.

Together in laughter, they find their peace,
As the world outside takes a quiet lease,
In the wild's corners, hearts collide,
Being solitary with fun as their guide.

The Tug of Unseen Branches

In a forest of shadows, they dance and sway,
Though I never quite see them, they play all day.
They whisper of secrets with a giggle or two,
Yet trip me with laughter when I don't have a clue.

I stumble through pathways, so lost in my thoughts,
The vines have a chuckle, my balance they've caught.
With each laugh they swing, they grab at my feet,
It's a comedy show—my own private feat!

Invisible friends in this jolly old glade,
They tease and they tug, in a playful charade.
I sense their delight with a chuckle and grin,
As I tumble and fumble, it's where I begin.

Amidst nature's jest, I find solace anew,
With branches of humor, ever clever and true.
In this tangled embrace, my heart finds a cheer,
These unseen companions, they keep me near.

Reverent Moments in Still Green

In a meadow where silence does humorously hum,
I trip over daisies; oh, here I go—dumb!
The stillness around me has a chuckle or two,
It seems even nature finds joy in my boo!

Whispers of wisdom float down from the trees,
But I'm busy attempting to swat at the bees.
They buzz like old friends having too good a time,
While I dance to their tune, looking quite out of rhyme.

Frogs croak in chorus, "Do the worm, it's a treat!"
While I wiggle and jiggle like I've got two left feet.
The flowers are laughing, their petals aflutter,
As I clumsily wander and sink in the butter.

Amidst all the laughter, I find my retreat,
With nature's sly giggles, I'm never complete.
In this stillness where chaos finds a clever spin,
These moments of joy are where the fun begins.

Beneath the Forgotten Canopy

I sit 'neath the leaves with a bowl of sweet cheer,
While squirrels tease me with their acorns so near.
They chatter in riddles, leaves twist with glee,
As I munch on my snacks, oblivious as can be.

The branches above me creak secrets of fun,
"I dare you to reach that!" says the mischievous one.
But I'm too busy munching, a ghost in my snack,
With crumbs on my lap, there's no turning back!

The tree trunks chuckle as I stand for a pose,
"Good luck getting down!" as my bravado so grows.
I wave to the bark like I'm king of this land,
But the roots roll their eyes; now I don't understand.

Their laughter surrounds me in this wild green space,
As I tumble and tumble, it's a laugh-a-minute race.
In a world of mistakes, find the humor inside,
Underneath the wide stretches, where cheerfulness hides.

The Longing of Forsaken Roots

Once rooted in place, but oh how I roam,
The ground calls my name, but my heart's made of foam.
I wander through laughter, I skip on a breeze,
While the roots shake their heads at my silly disease.

Every step is a jig, an impromptu affair,
While the grass gives a chuckle at my silly dare.
"Stay put!" they exclaim, but I laugh at their plight,
For dancing's my calling, and it feels so right!

In the arms of soft soil, I long to be free,
Yet the trees tease my spirit like they're mocking me.
"Come back!" says the moss as I whirl round and round,
But my funny little feet just can't stay on the ground.

With giggles and wobbles, I dream of the day,
When I'll join all the roots in a funnier way.
For every lost path leads to laughter so bold,
In the comedy of life, my heart finds its hold.

Fractured Roots of Longing

In a garden of dreams, I scowl,
Where weeds of wishful thinking grow.
I planted hopes with a frown,
But they just sprouted a disaster show.

The sun shines bright on my despair,
While snails take selfies down the lane.
I can't help but giggle at this affair,
As my longing dances in the rain.

My flowers refuse to bloom, oh dear!
They're on a strict procrastination plan.
I water them with bittersweet cheer,
And wonder why they hate me, man!

A squirrel throws a party in a pot,
Inviting all the seeds to play.
I'm left here tangled in this plot,
Laughing at my roots that went astray.

The Silent Embrace of Twilight

As daylight bids a sneaky goodbye,
I trip over shadows, oh what a sight!
The moon winks at the stars on high,
While I'm caught in an acrobatic fright.

A cat serenades the crickets' tune,
As fireflies throw a disco ball.
I wonder if they'll dance till noon,
While I'm stuck in a lyrical sprawl.

The air feels thick like an old cloud,
Just waiting for a dramatic drop.
I smile at all things oddly proud,
As night prepares to flip the shop.

In the quiet, I brew a silly thought,
Maybe twilight plays a trick on us.
But then again, chaos soon is sought,
A laugh in the dark is a must!

Gnarled Memories in Stillness

Where time forgot to speak a word,
Old trees shuffle secrets of the past.
Their gnarled limbs are a voice unheard,
In a park where echoes fade so fast.

I watch a squirrel play hide and seek,
As I reminisce about life's parade.
The memories come out, feeling weak,
Wrapped in laughter, like sunshine's braid.

Each twig has a story, or so they claim,
But their bark is worse than their bite!
I giggle as they speak of fame,
Among leaves that just can't take flight.

So I sit with the stillness of a bench,
Cracking jokes with the mist and trees.
In this silence, I don't feel a wrench,
For laughter flows with the morning breeze.

The Solace of a Leafless Canopy

Beneath the expanse of empty air,
In a park where branches forgot to grow,
I dance with nothing, quite the affair,
As the sun blinks down, putting on a show.

The sky yawns wide, in its solitude,
Dusted with tales of whimsy and fun.
I chuckle at the trees' crude attitude,
Who lost their leaves just to be done!

A crow caws out, quite the detective,
As I ponder the meaning of bare.
In this tree's loneliness, I feel reflective,
While giggling at how they all dare.

With every sway of the forgotten trunks,
The air fills with jokes of nature's grace.
In a world where silence still shrinks,
Finding solace feels like winning the race.

The Weight of Cedar's Solitude

In a forest where trees wear their woes,
A cedar sighed deeply, striking a pose.
"Why talk to the squirrels? They just make a fuss!"
Dropping acorns like wisdom, just to discuss.

A wise oak grinned wide, with its leaves all a'flutter,
'Your bark's quite amusing, but it could use some butter!'
The cedar just chuckled, filled with soft glee,
'I'll host my next party, just you wait and see!'

With shadows that dance and a laugh that's contagious,
The trees played charades, their humor outrageous.
"Does a tree never bark when it's feeling blue?"
"Nah, it just gives a nod, much like me and you."

So pine cones dropped jokes, and ferns rolled their eyes,
In this woodsy affair, beneath the clear skies.
Their chatter like whispers, a tickle of fun,
Who knew being lonely could be so well done?

Lullabies of Overshadowed Dreams

In the nook of the night, where shadows collide,
A whispering willow befriended her pride.
'We'll sing songs of sorrow, but also of cheer!'
Said the owl with a wink, 'I've got jokes we can hear.'

The stars twinkled brightly, a cosmic cabaret,
While crickets composed a rather odd play.
"Why don't secrets sleep? They'll just snore through the night!"
'Ah, they'd miss the good gossip, what a silly plight.'

Underneath the great moon, where dreams take a nap,
The tall grass kept giggling, plotting a trap.
"Let's sneak up on shadows, we'll tickle their toes!"
"Then run like the wind, just to see how it goes!"

So lullabies fluttered on wings of delight,
Embracing their oddness, defying the night.
With laughter like ripples across silver streams,
Life's a quirky dance, full of amusing dreams.

Flickering Embers of Lingering Light

A campfire once flickered, all cozy and round,
But it sparked up a party, oh what a sound!
"Why does the ember blush? Because it's got heat!"
Said the marshmallow chef, "it can't take a seat!"

With shadows a-jumping, and logs in a row,
The flames started chatting, putting on a show.
"Have you heard about wood that played jazz on the side?"
'Yeah, it's a real banger, it had quite the ride!'

The fireflies buzzed with their glow-worm parade,
"Join us on stage, don't be afraid!"
A flicker of laughter, with sparks flying high,
'The more that we giggle, the brighter we fly!'

In the warmth of this chaos, where laughter ignites,
The embers kept glowing through those starry nights.
Even shadows found joy in their jig and their sway,
'This solitude's fun, let's dance till the day!'

An Abode of Quiet Remembrance

In a cottage of memories, quite far from the fray,
An old cat with whiskers surveyed the array.
"Why do we sit here, in peace by the stove?"
Murmured a mouse, rolling his cheese like a globe.

The cat smirked, bemused, with a twitch of its tail,
"It's cozy in silence, we're hiding from trails."
"Besides," said the mouse, with a warm little grin,
"It's better than running; I'm feeling quite thin!"

As the clock ticked gently, a breeze made them sigh,
"How do you keep still when the world rushes by?"
"With a cup of warm tea and a good story, dear!"
The cat purred aloud, "we've nothing to fear!"

So in corners of calm, where the silence was sweet,
They chuckled on life with an attitude neat.
Memories fluttered like keys on a ring,
In the calm of remembrance, oh, the joy it can bring!

www.ingramcontent.com/pod-product-compliance
Lightning Source LLC
Chambersburg PA
CBHW052221090526
44585CB00015BA/1407